THE HEALING POWER OF GARLIC

Gayle Alleman, M.S., R.D.

Publications International, Ltd.

CHAPTER ONE
GARLIC'S GIFTS

The wonders of garlic have been with us for millennia. Writings from ancient Egypt, Greece, India, and China all make mention of the humble garlic clove. It has long been used in many cultures to improve health or transform meals into delicious, aromatic delights. Its ability to enhance flavor is undeniable, while the extent of its healing benefits continues to be revealed.

Garlic, or scientifically speaking, *Allium sativum*, is cultivated across the globe except in the polar regions. The bulb of this attractive plant contains more powerful sulfur compounds than does any other *Allium* species, such as onions or leeks. The garlic plant may have evolved to include these smelly sulfur compounds as a way of warding off foraging animals, invasive insects, and even soil-borne microorganisms such as bacteria and fungi. Yet these same compounds, which lend garlic its pungent aroma and delectable flavor, as well as its medicinal qualities, are exactly the reason so many people are attracted to the bulb.

FABLES AND FOLKLORE

Garlic, which has been grown for more than 5,000 years, is one of the oldest cultivated plants in the world. Researchers think the ancient Egyptians were the first to farm garlic; in fact, the little bulbs helped power the building of the Great Pyramids. Hard-working slaves received a ration of garlic each day to improve their strength and ward off illness. And a mere 15 pounds of this ancient currency would buy a

THE STINKING ROSE DIDN'T BLOOM FOR EVERYONE

For all of garlic's uses, the history of the "stinking rose" is not all rosy. In certain times and places, people despised garlic. During his reign in the 14th century, King Alphonso of Castile ordered people to stay away from him if they had eaten garlic within the past month. Its alleged aphrodisiac qualities made garlic taboo for Tibetan monks. Ancient Indians believed garlic would lure people away from spiritual endeavors, so it was banned in certain sacred places. What's more, the upper classes among them felt it would be barbaric to eat such a "common people's food." The British considered garlic rank, and even Shakespeare mentions it with disdain in several of his plays.

healthy male slave to add to the pyramid-building team. It seems fitting that garlic, a natural wonder with many healing and culinary properties, played a role in the creation of one of the wonders of the ancient world.

Ancient Egyptians attributed many sacred qualities to garlic. They believed it kept away evil spirits, so they buried garlic-shape lumps of clay with dead pharaohs. Archaeologists found preserved bulbs of garlic scattered around King Tut's tomb millennia after his burial.

The ancient Egyptians believed so strongly in the power of garlic to ward off evil spirits that they would chew it before making a journey at night. Garlic made them burp and gave them foul-smelling breath, creating a radius of odor so strong, they believed, that evil spirits would not penetrate it.

Ancient Greeks and Romans loved their garlic, too. Greek athletes and soldiers ate garlic before entering the arena or battlefield because they thought it had strength-enhancing properties. Roman soldiers ate garlic for inspiration and courage. Greek midwives hung garlic cloves in birthing rooms to repel evil spirits. Hippocrates, the ancient Greek known as the "father of medicine," prescribed garlic for a variety of ailments around 400 B.C. It was used to treat wounds, fight infection, cure leprosy, and ease digestive disorders. Other prominent Greeks used garlic to treat heart problems, as well.

Garlic's reputation as a medicinal wonder continued into the Middle Ages. It was used in attempts to prevent the plague and to treat leprosy and a long list of other ailments. Later, explorers and migrating peoples introduced this easy-to-grow and easy-to-carry plant to various regions around the world. The Spanish, Portuguese, and French introduced garlic to the Americas.

In many historic cultures, garlic was used medicinally but not in cooking. That might surprise us today, but were our ancestors able to travel into the future to visit us, they would likely think us rather dense for our culture's general lack of appreciation for the bulb's healing qualities.

Traditionally, garlic bulbs were prepared in a variety of ways for medicinal purposes. The juice of the bulb might be extracted and taken internally for one purpose, while the bulb might be ground into a paste for external treatment of other health problems. In the minds of the superstitious, simply possessing garlic was enough to bring good luck and protect against evil—especially evil in the form of mysterious and frightening entities, such as sorcerers and vampires.

GARLIC'S HISTORIC TARGETS

Garlic has been used throughout the ages to treat a long and varied list of ailments, including:

asthma
bladder infections
bronchitis
colds
colic
constipation
coughs
dandruff
diabetes
dysentery
earaches
eczema
fever
flatulence
flu
forgetfulness
gallbladder problems
graying of hair
hair loss
high blood pressure
indigestion
infections
infertility
insomnia
intestinal worms
liver problems
menstrual irregularities
paralysis
rabies
rheumatism
scabies
scorpion bites
seizures
sinus problems
tremors
tuberculosis
typhoid
ulcers
whooping cough

Legends convinced people that there were certain things over which vampires had no power, and garlic was one of them. However, it is only in European (and, by extension, American) folklore that vampires are powerless in the presence of garlic. The bulb apparently is not mentioned as a defensive tool against these infamous bloodsuckers in vampire legends from other parts of the world.

GARLIC MAKES THE HISTORY BOOKS

Garlic played its first starring role in modern medical treatment during World War I. The Russians used garlic on the front lines to treat battle wounds and fight infection, and medics used moss that was soaked in garlic as an antiseptic to pack wounds. In the first part of the 20th century, garlic saw plenty of action off the battlefield, too. Even though penicillin was discovered in 1928, the demand for it often outstripped the supply, so many people reverted to treatments they had used with some success before, including garlic.

The pungent, ancient remedy has found its way to modern times. Herbalists have long touted garlic for a number of health problems, from preventing colds and treating intestinal problems to lowering blood cholesterol and reducing heart-disease risk. Garlic remedies abound—and scientific research has begun to support the usefulness of some of them.

Garlic's popularity today is due in part to the efforts of scientists around the world. They have identified a number of sulfur-containing compounds in garlic that have important medicinal properties.

If you were to look at or sniff an intact garlic clove sitting on a cutting board, you'd never suspect the potent aroma and healing properties within. Whack it with a knife, however, and you open a portal. Cutting, crushing, or chewing a garlic clove activates numerous sulfurous substances. When these substances come into contact with oxygen, they form compounds that have therapeutic properties. The most researched, and possibly the most medicinally powerful, of these potent compounds are allicin and ajoene.

A Little Help for Your Heart

The tiny garlic clove may play a big role in reducing the risk of heart disease, heart attacks, and stroke. How could such a simple herb have such powerful, far-reaching effects? To explore the answer and gain some appreciation for garlic's labors on our behalf, it's important to have a basic understanding of how the heart functions in sickness and in health.

Heart disease is the number-one killer of Americans. The most common form of heart disease occurs when the arteries that deliver oxygen- and nutrient-rich blood to the heart become narrowed or clogged and lose their elasticity. Blood flow to the heart diminishes or may be cut off completely, starving the organ of oxygen. Without adequate oxygen, the heart can no longer work properly and heart cells begin to die.

Healthy arteries are similar to flexible tubes, wide open and able to contract and expand slightly as blood surges through with each heartbeat. When there is any injury to the inner lining of these vital tubes—such as damage caused by high blood cholesterol and triglyceride levels, high blood pressure, tobacco smoke, diabetes, and the aging process—the body tries to protect and heal the wounded area by producing a sticky substance to cover the damage.

This process is similar to the way we might use spackle to patch a small hole in drywall. But the sticky spackle the body produces to heal the wound causes fatty substances (including cholesterol), proteins, calcium, inflammatory cells, and other "debris" in the blood to stick to the vessel walls, forming plaque. As the plaque accumulates on the inner walls of the arteries, the arteries become less elastic, which leaves them vulnerable to even more injury. The

A Guide to Heart-Disease Terms

Antioxidant: A substance that inhibits oxidation, a natural body process that causes cell damage. The body uses vitamins C and E as antioxidants. It also uses the minerals selenium and manganese to build potent antioxidant defense mechanisms, such as glutathione peroxidase and superoxide dismutase, to protect your cells.

Arteriosclerosis: A disease in which the arteries have thickened, hardened, and lost their elasticity, resulting in impaired blood flow. It develops in people who have high blood pressure, high cholesterol, diabetes, and other conditions or as the result of aging. It is also known as "hardening of the arteries."

Atherosclerosis: A type of arteriosclerosis characterized by plaque deposits on the interior walls of arteries.

Fibrinolysis: The body's natural process of breaking up blood clots.

Homocysteine: A sulfur-containing amino acid in the blood that has been linked to an increased risk of premature coronary artery disease, stroke, and blood clots in the veins.

Hypercholesterolemia: High levels of cholesterol in the blood.

Hyperlipidemia: High levels of lipids in the blood.

Lipids: Another word for fats. Includes all types of cholesterol and triglycerides.

Nitric oxide: In the human body, nitric oxide plays a role in oxygen transport, nerve transmission, and other functions. It also helps relax the lining of the blood vessels.

Oxidation: A chemical reaction between oxygen and another substance, sometimes resulting in damage to the substance. For instance, oxidized cholesterol damages the lining of arteries.

gradual buildup of plaque also slowly narrows the inner diameter of the artery, and blood flow is hampered.

In addition, the plaque itself can crack, or bits of plaque can become dislodged. The body responds by sending platelets (particles in the blood that aid clotting) to form a clot around the plaque, further narrowing the artery. In some cases, the blood clot may completely block the flow of blood through the artery. Cells beyond the blockage that depend on a steady flow of oxygen from the blood can die. When this occurs in an artery that feeds the heart muscle (known as a coronary artery), it's called a heart attack. If this happens in a vessel that feeds the brain, the result is a stroke.

CHOLESTEROL'S ROLE IN HEART DISEASE

Some cholesterol is necessary for normal body processes—it forms a vital part of cell membranes, transports nutrients into and waste products out of cells, and is part of the structure of many hormones, among other functions—but too much of the wrong kind leads to trouble. A quick review of cholesterol will help you appreciate the beneficial role garlic might play in your heart's health.

Dietary cholesterol is a fatty substance, or lipid. When you eat cholesterol in food, as in meat, eggs, and cheese, your body breaks it down to digest it, then turns some of it back into cholesterol. Your body also makes cholesterol out of the solid fats (saturated fat and *trans* fat) in your diet.

Heredity also plays a role in the amount of cholesterol your body produces. Genetics determine whether your body makes a little or a lot of cholesterol from the fats you eat. If you have a family history of high blood cholesterol, your body may make large amounts of the substance regardless of your eating and activity habits.

All this cholesterol is transported throughout your body via your internal highway—the bloodstream. There are several types of blood cholesterol. The most significant are:

LDL cholesterol. LDL stands for low-density lipoprotein. LDL is nicknamed "bad" cholesterol because as it flows through your arteries it has a tendency to stick to the artery walls and form plaque. As the plaque builds up, it narrows the arteries. Arteries lined with plaque are no longer flexible and elastic. Instead, they are inflexible and "hard," which makes it more difficult for the heart to pump blood throughout the body. This increases your blood pressure and makes it harder for the blood to deliver oxygen and nutrients to your body.

HDL cholesterol. HDL stands for high-density lipoprotein. HDL carries the nickname "good" cholesterol because it works to eliminate excess blood cholesterol so it doesn't collect in the arteries and increase your risk for heart attacks and strokes. HDL carries cholesterol to the liver, where it is metabolized and then eliminated from the body. The higher your HDL level, the lower your chance of getting heart disease.

HEART-HEALTHY GARLIC

Many studies have tried to determine whether—and how—garlic plays a role in keeping your ticker in tip-top shape. Research indicates that garlic plays a significant part in:

- Lowering blood pressure
- "Thinning" the blood
- Lowering triglycerides
- Lowering "bad" LDL cholesterol
- Breaking up blood clots
- Relaxing blood vessel walls and protecting them from damage

Triglycerides. Triglycerides are another form of lipid. Although they are not cholesterol, they do adversely affect your heart's health if you have too many in your blood. They can contribute to the thickening of artery walls. Your body manufactures triglycerides, and they are also present in food.

GARLIC'S IMPACT ON BLOOD CHOLESTEROL LEVELS

You've probably seen advertisements for garlic supplements and debated whether you should eat more garlic to improve your heart's health. Perhaps you've wondered if it's worth the odor or if it's only good for keeping vampires at bay. Does garlic really promote heart health, and if so, how?

Research on animals and humans in the 1980s and early 1990s seemed to indicate that garlic had much promise for lowering cholesterol. It appeared that garlic was able to

KNOW YOUR NUMBERS

Here are the optimal blood lipid levels from the National Heart, Lung, and Blood Institute (as of 2005):

- *Total cholesterol:* 200 milligrams of cholesterol per deciliter of blood (mg/dL) or less
- *LDL cholesterol:* 100 mg/dL or less
- *HDL cholesterol:* 40 mg/dL or more
- *Triglycerides:* 150 mg/dL or less

Note: Cholesterol levels are just one of several risk factors, including family history and smoking, that add up to determine your risk of heart disease. If you have one or more risk factors, you may need to aim for lipid levels lower than the standard ones listed here. Check with your health-care provider.

lower total blood cholesterol in those who had high blood cholesterol (levels of 200 mg/dL or more). However, many of the studies included small numbers of patients and were short term, lasting just three months or less.

A number of more recent studies have tempered the initial enthusiasm about garlic's cholesterol-lowering effects. The National Center for Complementary and Alternative Medicine, a division of the National Institutes of Health (NIH), requested a thorough review of human studies that investigated garlic's ability to control cholesterol levels. The NIH released a paper in 2000 that concluded garlic did not alter HDL, but that it could significantly lower LDL cholesterol and triglycerides in the short term. Researchers determined that garlic had the greatest cholesterol-lowering effect in the first one to three months of garlic therapy. After six months, no further lipid reductions occurred.

Elevated cholesterol levels, however, contribute to heart disease over a long period of time. So based on this newer research, it would appear that although garlic may be a helpful addition to a cholesterol-lowering diet, it can't be relied upon as the sole solution to high blood cholesterol levels.

Still, it's obvious that more research is needed. Indeed, the NIH statement in 2000 encouraged longer-term studies, as well as consideration of the type of garlic used. For example, there is some evidence that garlic must be cut or crushed to activate its health-promoting components. But the products tested in the various studies were not consistent. Some used raw garlic, while others used dried garlic or garlic oil; sometimes the raw garlic was cut, sometimes it was minced, and sometimes it was used whole. When dried garlic was used, it often was made into a powder and formed into tablets. It's also unknown whether garlic just stops being effective after several months or whether other factors in these studies influenced the findings.

THE BOTTOM LINE: GARLIC AND CHOLESTEROL

Although garlic may not be the blood-cholesterol miracle cure it was once promoted to be, and there are still plenty of questions that require answers, garlic does appear to have a healing role to play. A 2005 Mayo Clinic report gave garlic a grade of "B" for small reductions in blood cholesterol and LDL cholesterol over short periods of time (4 to 12 weeks). A "B" grade means there is good scientific evidence to support its use for that purpose. The Mayo Clinic reported the following findings from multiple studies:

- Supplements of nonenteric-coated tablets containing dehydrated garlic powder (standardized to 1.3 percent alliin) may reduce total cholesterol by up to 20 mg/dL for 4 to 12 weeks. The effects are unclear beyond 20 weeks.

- LDL may decrease by up to 10 mg/dL.

- Triglycerides may decrease by up to 20 mg/dL.

- HDL cholesterol levels are not significantly affected.

Mayo's report concluded that well-designed studies of longer duration and including more people might provide stronger evidence of garlic's cholesterol-reducing benefits. In the meantime, however, garlic is not likely to take the place of medications prescribed by a physician to lower blood cholesterol levels.

On the other hand, doctors often recommend that patients try lifestyle changes to lower cholesterol levels before or even along with drug therapy. Drugs often come with side effects—some merely unpleasant, others downright dangerous—and postponing or minimizing drug therapy with lifestyle changes can cut the risks of such side effects. Garlic's main drawback seems to be the odor it gives your breath and perspiration. Although garlic should never take the place of prescribed medications, including it more often in a cholesterol-lowering diet is easy, inexpensive, and enhances the flavor of your meals—especially those that are low in fat and sodium.

MORE WAYS THAT GARLIC WINS YOUR HEART

Luckily for us, nature packaged the equivalent of a chemical factory inside every little garlic clove. In addition to potent

DIFFERENT FORMS OF GARLIC YIELD DIFFERENT RESULTS

One of the difficulties in comparing studies of garlic's effectiveness in humans is that there are many different forms of garlic used in the studies. One may contain more of an active ingredient than another. For example:

◆ *Fresh cloves of garlic—chopped or chewed:* These may impart the highest amount of allicin, but they have not been well studied yet.

◆ *Fresh cloves of garlic—swallowed whole:* These showed no therapeutic value in a limited number of studies that have been done.

◆ *Dehydrated garlic powder—made into tablets or capsules:* This form often provided some therapeutic value, but allicin content of these products varies within and among brands.

◆ *Enteric-coated garlic tablets:* These are treated so they do not dissolve until they reach your intestines, rather than your stomach. Some studies show that enteric-coated tablets don't dissolve soon enough to release their allicin, but they do prevent garlic breath.

◆ *Nonenteric-coated garlic tablets:* Tablets effective in studies were standardized to contain 1.3 percent allicin (more about the content of garlic supplements later). These may be more effective than the enteric-coated tablets, but they cause garlic breath.

◆ *Aged garlic extract:* The active compound in this form is ajoene, among others. There have been conflicting results in studies of health benefits.

◆ *Garlic oil:* Shows little therapeutic value in studies.

sulfur compounds such as allicin, garlic has other secrets in its heart-disease-fighting arsenal.

GARLIC'S ATTACK ON PLAQUE

Garlic contains several powerful antioxidants—compounds that prevent oxidation, a harmful process in the body. One of them is selenium, a mineral that is a component of glutathione peroxidase, a powerful antioxidant that the body makes to defend itself. Glutathione peroxidase works with vitamin E to form a superantioxidant defense system.

Other antioxidants in garlic include vitamin C, which helps reduce the damage that LDL cholesterol can cause, and quercetin, a phytochemical. (Phytochemicals are chemical substances found in plants that may have health benefits for people.) Garlic also has trace amounts of the mineral manganese, which is an important component of an antioxidant enzyme called superoxide dismutase.

Oxidation is related to oxygen, an element vital to every aspect of our lives, so why is oxidation so harmful? Think about when rust accumulates on your car or garden tools and eventually destroys the metal. That rust is an example of oxidation. Similarly, when your body breaks down glucose for energy, free radicals are produced. These free radicals start oxidizing—and damaging—cellular tissue. It's as if your bloodstream and blood vessels are "rusting out."

Antioxidants destroy free radicals, including those that are products of environmental factors, such as ultraviolet rays, air pollutants, cigarette smoke, rancid oils, and pesticides. The body keeps a steady supply of antioxidants ready to neutralize free radicals. Unfortunately, sometimes the number of free radicals can overwhelm the body's antioxidant stock, especially if we're not getting enough of the antioxidant nutrients.

When free radicals harm the cells that line your arteries, your body tries to mend the damage by producing a sticky spackle-like substance. However, as mentioned earlier, this substance attracts cholesterol and debris that build up within the arteries, causing progressive plaque formation. The more plaque in your arteries, the more your health is in danger.

In addition, the cholesterol circulating through your arteries can be oxidized by free radicals. When LDL is oxidized, it damages the lining of the arteries, which significantly contributes to the buildup of plaque and the narrowing and hardening of the arteries.

Arteries, then, benefit greatly from the protection antioxidants provide. And garlic's ability to stop the oxidation of cholesterol may be one of the many ways it protects heart health.

Garlic also appears to help prevent calcium from binding with other substances that lodge themselves in plaque. In a UCLA Medical Center study, 19 people were given either a placebo or an aged garlic extract that contained S-allylcysteine, one of garlic's sulfur-rich compounds, for one year. The placebo group had a significantly greater increase in their calcium score (22.2 percent) than the group that received the aged garlic extract (calcium score of 7.5 percent). The results of this small pilot study suggest that aged garlic extract may inhibit the rate of coronary artery calcification. If further larger-scale studies confirm these results, garlic may prove to be a useful preventative tool for patients at high risk of future cardio-vascular problems.

EASING THE PRESSURE

Research suggests garlic can help make small improvements in blood pressure by increasing the blood flow to the capillaries, which are the tiniest blood vessels. The chemicals in garlic achieve this by causing the capillary walls to open wider and reducing the ability of blood platelets to stick together and cause blockages. Reductions are small—10 mmHg (millimeters of mercury, the unit of measurement for blood pressure) or less. This means if your blood pressure is 130 over 90 mmHg, garlic *might* help lower it to 120 over 80 mmHg. That's a slight improvement, but, along with some simple lifestyle adjustments, such as getting more exercise, garlic might help move your blood pressure out of the danger zone.

Preliminary studies indicate that garlic may also increase the production of nitric oxide. This chemical compound is produced in the lining of blood vessels, and it helps the vessels relax and allow blood to flow more freely. Research published in August 2005 in the *Proceedings of the National Academy of Sciences* indicates that some of the sulfur-rich compounds in garlic help blood vessels relax and enlarge, lowering blood pressure and improving blood flow throughout the body.

THE BOTTOM LINE:
GARLIC AND HEART HEALTH

Garlic seems to deserve a spot on the battlefield in the fight against heart disease. Even if its lipid-lowering abilities are less extensive than once thought, it appears that garlic's antioxidant ability helps protect arteries from plaque formation and eventual blockage. Because garlic also appears to increase the nitric oxide in vessels and lower your blood pressure, it becomes even more valuable.

INFECTION FIGHTER

Garlic's potential to combat heart disease has received a lot of attention, but it should receive even more acclaim for its antimicrobial properties. Fresh, raw garlic has proven itself since ancient times as an effective killer of bacteria and viruses. Once again, we can thank allicin.

Laboratory studies confirm that raw garlic has antibacterial and antiviral properties. Not only does it knock out many common cold and flu viruses, but its effectiveness also spans a broad range of both gram-positive and gram-negative bacteria (two major classifications of bacteria), fungus, intestinal parasites, and yeast. Cooking garlic, however, destroys the allicin, so you'll need to use raw garlic to prevent or fight infections.

ANTIMICROBIAL ACTIVITY

Garlic's infection-fighting capability was confirmed in a study conducted by researchers at the University of Ottawa that was published in the April 2005 issue of *Phytotherapy Research*. Researchers tested 19 natural health products that contain garlic and five fresh garlic extracts for active compounds and antimicrobial activity. They tested the effectiveness of these substances against three types of common bacteria: *E. faecalis*, which causes urinary tract infections; *N. gonorrhoeae*, which causes the sexually transmitted disease gonorrhea; and *S. aureus*, which is responsible for many types of infections that are common in hospitals. The products most successful at eradicating these bacteria were the ones with the highest allicin content.

Now garlic is being investigated to see whether it can help us battle microbes that are resistant to antibiotics.

One simple but meaningful demonstration of garlic's anti-bacterial power can be found in a study conducted at the University of California, Irvine. Garlic juice was tested in the laboratory against a wide spectrum of potential pathogens, including several antibiotic-resistant strains of bacteria. It showed significant activity against the pathogens. Even more exciting was the fact that garlic juice still retained significant antimicrobial activity, even in dilutions ranging up to 1:128 of the original juice.

Is it possible that garlic can work alongside prescription medications to both reduce side effects and to help the drugs work better? Results from several studies say yes.

In a Rutgers University study that used bacteria in lab dishes, garlic and two common antibiotics were pitted against certain antibiotic-resistant strains of *S. aureus* (a gram-positive bacteria) and *E. coli* (a gram-negative bacteria). Garlic was able to significantly increase the effectiveness of the two antibiotic medications in killing the bacteria.

Research done in Mexico City at a facility supported by the National Institutes of Health of Mexico also showed some interesting results. It extended previous research in rats that used aged garlic extract and various sulfur-containing compounds from garlic along with gentamicin, a powerful antibiotic that can cause kidney damage. When any of the garlic compounds was ingested along with gentamicin, kidney damage was diminished.

Next, researchers set about to determine whether garlic weakened the effectiveness of gentamicin. As it turns out, the exact opposite happened: Garlic actually *enhanced* the effect of gentamicin. These findings indicate that with the use of garlic, perhaps less gentamicin would be needed, and kidney damage could be minimized.

Judging by research conducted in lab dishes and animals, it appears that garlic is a strong defender against microbes, even against those that have developed a resistance to common antibiotics. It also appears that garlic enhances the effects of some traditional antibiotics. But does it stand up to the test in humans?

BATTLING THE BUGS WITHIN

Eating raw garlic may help combat the sickness-causing bugs that get loose inside our bodies. Garlic has been used internally as a folk remedy for years, but now the plant is being put to the test scientifically for such uses. So far, its grades are quite good as researchers pit it against a variety of bacteria.

For eons, herbalists loaded soups and other foods with garlic and placed garlic compresses on people's chests to provide relief from colds and chest congestion. Now the Mayo Clinic has stated, "Preliminary reports suggest that garlic may reduce the severity of upper respiratory tract infection." The findings have not yet passed the scrutiny of numerous, large, well-designed human studies, so current results are classified as "unclear."

Can a garlic clove help stop your sniffles? A study published in the July/August 2001 issue of *Advances in Therapy* examined the stinking rose's ability to fight the common cold. The study involved 146 volunteers divided into two groups. One group took a garlic supplement for 12 weeks during the winter months, while the other group received a placebo. The group that received garlic had significantly fewer colds—and the colds that they did get went away faster—than the placebo group.

Garlic also may help rid the intestinal tract of Giardia lamblia, a parasite that commonly lives in stream water and causes giardiasis, an infection of the small intestine. Hikers and campers run the risk of this infection whenever they drink untreated stream or lake water. Herbalists prescribe a solution of one or more crushed garlic cloves stirred into one-third of a cup of water taken three times a day to eradicate Giardia. If you're fighting giardiasis, be sure to consult your health-care provider, because it's a nasty infection. Ask if you can try garlic as part of your treatment.

Finally, in the January 2005 issue of *Antimicrobial Agents and Chemotherapy*, researchers reported the results of an investigation into whether fresh garlic extract would inhibit *C. albicans*, a cause of yeast infections. The extract was very effective in the first hour of exposure to *C. albicans*, but the effectiveness decreased during the 48-hour period it was measured. However, conventional antifungal medications have the same declining effectiveness as time passes.

EXTERNAL TREATMENTS

Garlic has many uses on the outside of the body, too. Applying a topical solution of raw garlic and water may stop wounds from getting infected. (Simply crush one clove of garlic and mix it with one-third of a cup of clean water. Use the solution within three hours because it will lose its potency over time.) A garlic solution used as a footbath several times a day is traditionally believed to improve athlete's foot.

FOUR THIEVES' VINEGAR

There are about as many versions of the four thieves' vinegar story as there are recipes for the concoction. One popular version, reported to be from the Parliament of Toulouse archives of 1628–1631, goes like this: Four thieves living in Marseilles, France, during the 17th century plagues were convicted of going to the houses of plague victims and robbing them, but the thieves themselves never became ill. To receive a lesser sentence they revealed their secret—they protected themselves by consuming daily doses of a mixture that contained vinegar, garlic, and a handful of other herbs. Those in charge were so grateful that they hanged the four thieves, rather than burning them at the stake.

A study conducted at Bastyr University, a natural health sciences school and research center near Seattle, showed that a garlic oil extract cured all warts it was applied to within two weeks. A water extract of garlic was much less effective. In the same study, the garlic oil extract also proved useful in dissolving corns.

Using garlic oil extract appears to work better than the old folk remedy of tying or taping a slice of garlic to a wart. If the slice of garlic is bigger than the wart or moves just a bit, it blisters the healthy surrounding skin (of course, you have the same risk when using wart-removing products that contain acid). Garlic's phytochemical compounds are strong enough to create chemical burns, so always apply externally with caution and do not use on young children. One way you can protect the surrounding healthy skin is to smear petroleum jelly on it before you apply the garlic.

Cancer Crusader

Some scientists think garlic may be able to help prevent one of the most dreaded maladies—cancer. The Mayo Clinic has reported that some studies using cancer cells in the laboratory, as well as some studies with animals and people, have suggested that eating garlic, especially unprocessed garlic, might reduce the risk of stomach and colon cancers.

The National Institutes of Health's National Cancer Institute drew similar conclusions after reviewing 37 studies involving garlic and sulfur-containing compounds. Twenty-eight of those studies indicated garlic possessed at least some anti-cancer activity, especially toward prostate and stomach cancer. Because the studies in question were merely observational (they compared people who reported eating a lot of garlic to those who did not), more studies are needed.

Still, the research the National Cancer Institute reviewed found that it may not take much garlic to reap these anti-cancer benefits. Eating as few as two servings of garlic a week might be enough to help protect against colon cancer. Controlled clinical trials will help determine the true extent of garlic's cancer-fighting powers.

What gives garlic these wonderful gifts? Several factors, including antioxidants and those same sulfur-containing agents we've discussed before, including allicin. (Antioxidants help protect cells from damage; continual cell damage can eventually lead to cancer.) Allicin appears to protect colon cells from the toxic effects of cancer-causing agents. For instance, when meat is cooked with garlic, the herb reduces the production of cancer-causing compounds that would otherwise form when meat is grilled at high temperatures.

GARLIC'S
ANTI-INFLAMMATORY PROPERTIES

Inflammation is the body's reaction to an injury, irritation, or infection. The symptoms of inflammation include redness, swelling, and pain.

Whenever the body suffers an injury, it sends many substances to the site to begin the healing process and to fight off foreign invaders, such as bacteria that can cause infections. Inflammation is so vigorous in its duties that sometimes the surrounding tissues get damaged. This can occur at the site of a wound, inside blood vessels that have succumbed to an injury by oxidized LDL cholesterol, or in airways that are exposed to something that irritates them.

Certain complexes in garlic appear to help minimize the body's inflammatory response. By decreasing inflammation, garlic may lend a hand by doing the following:

- Protecting the inside of your arteries
- Reducing the severity of asthma
- Protecting against inflammation in the joints, such as in rheumatoid arthritis and osteoarthritis
- Reducing inflammation in nasal passages and airways, such as that associated with colds

Garlic's potential ability to decrease *H. pylori* bacteria in the stomach may help prevent gastritis (inflammation of the stomach lining) from eventually evolving into cancer. (*H. pylori* is most famous for its link to stomach ulcers, but it can also cause chronic gastritis.) Numerous studies around the world indicate that garlic's sulfur-containing compounds have the potential to help prevent stomach cancer.

The American Institute for Cancer Research (AICR), an organization that supports research into the roles diet and nutrition play in the prevention and treatment of cancer, has cited two large studies—one in China and the other in Italy—in which garlic intake was associated with lower death rates from stomach cancer. In addition, a Korean study indicated garlic consumption led to a lower risk of developing stomach cancer. And the AICR has reported that the Iowa Women's Health Study revealed that women had a lower risk of colon cancer if they ate garlic regularly. (The report did not define what amount and frequency constituted regular use.)

The amount of garlic you eat, along with the number of years you eat it regularly, may determine its ability to decrease cancer risk. This makes sense because cancer takes a long time to develop. In general, researchers suspect that garlic delivers anticancer benefits if you eat substantial amounts of it for three to five years or longer (again, the report did not define how much garlic should be eaten). That's when they begin to see a possible link in the reduction of laryngeal, gastric, colon, and endometrial (uterine) cancers.

Most studies do not show a reduction in breast cancer risk related to garlic intake. The data about whether garlic helps prevent development of prostate cancer is less definitive. And in a preliminary study that looked at consumption of fruits and vegetables, garlic appeared to be the only variable that might slightly decrease the risk of ovarian cancer; clearly, however, more studies are needed.

FIGHTING THE COMMON COLD

Herbalists recommend chewing garlic and holding it in your mouth for a while before swallowing it to obtain the best dose of bacteria-fighting allicin. This may be rather difficult for children or for those who find garlic to be too spicy. As an alternative, mince a clove, let it sit for 10 to 15 minutes so the allicin can form, then stuff it into empty gelatin capsules (which you can purchase in the herb section of a natural foods store). Taking three cloves a day when you have a cold may help you feel better. If the raw garlic bothers your stomach, take the capsules with food that contains a little bit of canola oil or, better yet, olive oil.

Other folk remedies battle colds and chest congestion with a garlic poultice or plaster. To make one, put some chopped garlic in a clean cloth, thin washcloth, or paper towel. Fold it over to enclose the garlic. Pour very warm (but not hot) water over the wrapped garlic, let it sit for a few seconds, and then lightly wring it out. Place the wrapped garlic on the chest for several minutes. Reheat with very warm water and place on the back, over the lung area, for several minutes. Some herbalists also recommend placing the poultice on the soles of the feet.

Caution: Be careful not to let garlic come into direct contact with the skin. Cut garlic is so powerful that prolonged exposure to the skin may result in a burn.

Garlic might defend against skin cancer when applied topically to tumors. In a study that appeared in the July 2003 issue of *Archives of Dermatological Research*, ajoene significantly shrunk skin cancer tumors in 17 out of 21 patients. The AICR has reported that in laboratory studies, the garlic compounds diallyl disulfide and ajoene protect against skin cancer.

Don't try treating skin cancer or unidentified/suspect skin lesions with garlic yourself, however. Skin cancer is a serious disease, and if you have it or suspect it, you should be following your physician's treatment guidelines. If you have a suspicious lesion, bring it to your physician's attention before using any home remedies.

TREATING YEAST INFECTIONS

One of the traditional ways women have self-treated vaginal yeast infections is by carefully peeling a clove of garlic without nicking it, wrapping it in a small piece of gauze, and inserting it into the vagina overnight. The garlic is removed in the morning, and the treatment is repeated for the next several nights, until 24 hours after symptoms diminish. There hasn't been any scientific research done to confirm that this home remedy works, but many women have used it for yeast infection relief for many years.

A LOOK INSIDE A CLOVE

A clove of garlic a day is often the amount recommended for medicinal purposes. Garlic contains an array of nutrients, but vitamins and minerals aren't the only health-bestowing substances present. Phytochemicals, naturally occurring chemicals that plants produce, abound in garlic. Many of them contain sulfur and have been highlighted earlier. Here is a look at some of the essential nutrients within a single clove.

CALORIES	4.5

MACRONUTRIENTS

Carbohydrate	<1 g
Fat	<1 g
Protein	<1 g
Fiber	0.06 g

VITAMINS

Thiamin (B_1)	0.01 mg
Riboflavin (B_2)	0.01 mg
Niacin equivalents	0.05 mg
Vitamin B_6	0.04 mg
Vitamin C	0.94 mg
Folate	0.09 mcg

MINERALS

Calcium	5.43 mg
Copper	0.01 mg
Iron	0.05 mg
Magnesium	0.75 mg
Manganese	0.05 mg
Phosphorus	4.59 mg
Potassium	12.03 mg
Selenium	0.43 mcg
Sodium	0.51 mg
Zinc	0.03 mg

g = grams mg = milligrams (0.001 grams) mcg = micrograms (0.000001 grams)

GARLIC'S SAFETY

Garlic is safe for most adults. Other than that special aroma garlic lends to your breath and perspiration, the herb has few side effects. However, you should know about a few cautions:

◆ If you are allergic to plants in the Liliaceae (lily) family, including onions, leeks, chives, and such flowers as hyacinth and tulip, avoid garlic. People who are allergic to garlic may have reactions whether it's taken by mouth, inhaled, or applied to the skin.

◆ People anticipating surgery or dental procedures, pregnant women, and those with bleeding disorders should avoid taking large amounts of garlic on a regular basis due to its ability to "thin" the blood, which could cause excessive bleeding. Taking blood thinners such as warfarin (brand name Coumadin) or aspirin and other nonsteroidal anti-inflammatory drugs (such as ibuprofen or naproxen) along with garlic is not recommended, unless you first discuss it with your health-care provider so dosing adjustments can be made. To be safe, if you have any questions about your use of garlic, talk with your health-care provider.

◆ Garlic interferes with medications other than anticoagulants. Garlic may interact with and affect the action of birth control pills, cyclosporine (often prescribed for rheumatoid arthritis), and some other medications. It also interferes with certain HIV/AIDS antiviral medications, reducing their effectiveness. Talk with your health-care provider and/or pharmacist if you take prescription medications and regularly eat large amounts of garlic or take any type of garlic supplement.

◆ Nursing women may find that garlic gives their milk an "off" flavor that the baby may reject, resulting in shorter nursing times.

◆ Consuming large amounts of garlic can irritate the stomach lining and possibly cause heartburn, abdominal pain, flatulence, diarrhea, or constipation. Go easy with garlic if you have a sensitive stomach.

◆ If applied directly to the skin, garlic can cause burns. Be especially careful using raw garlic on children's skin.

The Skinny on Supplements

Fresh, naturally grown raw garlic is best, but if you can't get enough of it into your diet, here is the scoop on supplements.

As noted in several of the research studies mentioned, not all garlic supplements consistently have the amount of allicin claimed on the label when they undergo testing. There are many possible variables, including differences in the garlic itself, growing conditions, amounts and types of fertilizer, type of garlic, the processing methods used, and quality control during manufacturing.

This remains a problem with assessing research on garlic— do the commercial garlic preparations contain what they say they do? Which compounds do they really have and how much is there in the supplement you're taking?

Supplements are typically made by slicing garlic and drying it at low temperatures to prevent the destruction of alliinase, the enzyme that turns alliin into the disease-fighter allicin. It is then pulverized into a powder and formed into tablets. In order to meet the standards set by the U.S. Pharmacopeia (the group that develops the quality standards for prescription and over-the-counter drugs and dietary supplements sold in the United States), the powder must contain at least 0.3 percent alliin.

Because manufacturers process and label their supplements differently, shopping for garlic supplements can be confusing. Some tablets do not contain any allicin, but rather alliin, which is converted to allicin. Other tablets contain both alliin and allicin. And some supplement labels may have an "allicin potential" or "allicin yield" statement. This refers to the amount of allicin that *could* be formed when alliin is converted, not how much allicin is *actually* formed.

In addition, because the enzyme alliinase is destroyed by the strong acidic conditions in the stomach, most supplements are "enteric coated" to keep them from dissolving until they reach the small intestine. Most tablets tested, though, produce only a little allicin under these tough conditions, and the tablets often take too long to dissolve. The better measurement is "allicin release." This discloses how much allicin the supplement actually produces under conditions similar to those found in the digestive tract. However, only a few manufacturers list this measurement on their labels.

With all this in mind, you should start by looking for the "standardization" statement on a label when choosing a garlic supplement—but even this isn't a foolproof guarantee. When a product is "standardized," it is supposed to have a certain amount of a specific ingredient. For instance, a product that says, "standardized to contain 1.3 percent alliin" means that every pill in every bottle should contain at least 1.3 percent alliin. Unfortunately, this is not always the case, but a product that carries the USP (U.S. Pharmacopeia) seal follows set methods to help ensure standardization.

Allicin is not the only active compound in garlic, but the other compounds are typically not standardized. Thus, you often don't know everything you're getting when purchasing a supplement.

EAR INFECTION THERAPY

Garlic extract added to olive oil is an age-old remedy for ear infections. Herbalists recommend slightly heating the oil, adding a very small amount of sliced garlic, letting it sit for a few minutes, and then straining it thoroughly before putting a couple of drops into the infected ear. There must be absolutely no garlic particles in the oil.

Before you place the oil in the ear, place a few drops on the inside of your arm and let it sit for several minutes to be sure that it is not strong enough to burn your arm (either because of the temperature of the oil or the amount of garlic essence present). If it passes the test, put a few small drops into the infected ear. Make a fresh batch for each treatment.

It's safest to check with your health-care provider before trying this home remedy, and it is essential if you have or have ever had a ruptured eardrum.

Which kind of supplement is best? Dried garlic powder is considered to have effects similar to those of fresh, crushed garlic. Other types of supplements, such as oils from crushed garlic, aged garlic extract in alcohol, and steam-distilled oils seem to contain less allicin and perhaps less of other active compounds than the dried powder.

When shopping for a garlic supplement, look for one that indicates it is standardized to contain at least 1.3 percent allicin. In the United States, pharmacy-grade garlic contains

0.3 percent (powdered form) to 0.5 percent (fresh, dried form) allicin. Avoid enteric-coated or time-release tablets because these may not dissolve soon enough in your digestive tract to make use of the allicin.

HOW MUCH SHOULD YOU TAKE?

Large scientific boards make several recommendations about daily garlic dosage. The Mayo Clinic cites the European Scientific Cooperative on Phytotherapy's recommendation for prevention of atherosclerosis as 3 milligrams to 5 milligrams allicin (3,000 micrograms to 5,000 micrograms allicin) or one clove or 0.5 gram to 1 gram of dried powder.

The World Health Organization recommends 2 grams to 5 grams of fresh garlic, 0.4 gram to 1.2 grams of dried garlic powder, 2 milligrams to 5 milligrams of garlic oil, 300 milligrams to 1,000 milligrams of garlic extract, or some other formulation that yields the equivalent of 2 milligrams to 5 milligrams (2,000 to 5,000 micrograms) of allicin daily.

GO TO THE CLOVE

Rather than fussing over garlic supplements that may or may not contain what they claim, just enjoy the heady aroma and flavor of fresh garlic in the foods you eat. You'll always know you're getting the best—and the most potent—allicin you can when you add garlic to foods. Consider this:

◆ A typical garlic clove weighs about 3 grams.

◆ The amount of alliin in an average clove ranges from 24 milligrams to 56 milligrams.

THE BOTTOM LINE

◆ Aim for about 5 milligrams of allicin per day.

◆ Use supplements that state the amount of "allicin release" rather than "allicin yield" or "allicin potential."

◆ When reading supplement labels, note that the amount of allicin is often listed in micrograms (mcg) rather than milligrams (mg). There are 1,000 micrograms in 1 milligram, so a supplement that contains 5,000 micrograms of allicin has 5 milligrams of allicin, which meets the European Scientific Cooperative on Phytotherapy's recommendation of 3 to 5 milligrams of allicin.

◆ A supplement may contain 500 milligrams of dried garlic bulb, which is equal to 0.5 gram. This falls into the low end of the World Health Organization's recommendation for dried garlic powder. Remember that dried powder contains just a small amount of allicin. Other compounds make up the rest of the tablet.

◆ A standard clove will produce about 2.5 milligrams to 4.5 milligrams of allicin per gram of fresh weight when crushed. This means you'll get 7.5 milligrams to 13.5 milligrams of allicin from one typical clove that weighs 3 grams.

What else on your plate delivers such a punch of healing power in such a small and flavorful package?

CHAPTER TWO
GARLIC: A CULINARY DELIGHT

The type of garlic you choose and how you prepare and use it combine to determine its healing properties and flavor. This chapter will show you how to make the most of your garlic, and enjoy every bit—and bite—of it.

Beautiful garlic braids decorate many kitchens. Some are adorned with peppers or dried flowers, while others sport a country ribbon. But garlic's role in the kitchen shouldn't be limited to wall decor. With a peel and a chop, garlic adds an aroma and flavor that few ingredients can match. This modest herb enlivens the kitchen, enchanting at least three of our senses.

Chefs all over the world put garlic to work in their kitchens. And a little clove really gets down to business. Not only does garlic boost the flavor of other foods but it also possesses many healthful and healing properties.

Garlic plays the role of star or supporting cast member equally well, whether it's used in appetizers, main courses, side dishes, drinks, or even desserts. Don't be shy about adding it almost anywhere. If you're not sure how, where, and when to use garlic, keep reading! The tips in this section will help you get to know garlic in the most intimate and delicious ways.

GARLIC VARIETIES

Garlic, garlic, hanging on the wall, which of you is the best of all? The first step to a perfect meal is selecting the ideal bulb from the more than 400 species and varieties of garlic. *Allium sativum* is the most common type of garlic; it is the one you'll typically find in the grocery store and is often called "culinary" garlic. Fortunately, this is the species that also offers the most healing properties.

You might occasionally find *Allium ursinum* in specialty or farmer's markets. *Allium ursinum* is a type of wild garlic native to Northern Europe that does not possess the same healing properties as *Allium sativum*. You might also come across *Allium vineale*, a garlic with very small cloves that is commonly called "crow garlic." This variety is nothing more than a weed.

Allium sativum has two subvarieties: softneck and hardneck. The two types have similar healing properties because they belong to the same species, but they differ in flavor, clove size, shelf life, and use.

SOFTNECK GARLIC

Softneck garlic is the type you'll most likely see in the produce section of your grocery store. Its name comes from the multilayered parchment that covers the entire bulb, continues up the neck of the bulb, and forms a soft, pliable stalk suitable for braiding. Its papery skin, or sheath, is a beautiful creamy white color.

Softneck garlic typically has several layers of cloves surrounding the central portion of the garlic bulb. The outermost layer's cloves are the stoutest; the cloves of the internal layers become smaller closer to the center of the bulb. Of the several types of softneck garlic, two are most abundant:

Silverskin garlic. This easy-to-grow variety has a strong flavor and stores well when dried—it will last nearly a year under the right conditions. The Creole group of silverskin garlics has a rose-tinted parchment.

Artichoke garlic. Artichoke garlic has a milder flavor and may have fewer and larger cloves than silverskin. You can store it as long as eight months. Artichoke garlic may occasionally have purple spots or streaks on its skin, but don't confuse it with purple stripe garlic, a hardneck variety that has quite a bit of purple coloring.

HARDNECK GARLIC

Unlike softneck garlic, hardneck varieties do not have a flexible stalk. When you buy this type of garlic, it will typically have an extremely firm stalk protruding an inch or two from the top of the bulb.

Hardneck garlic sends up scapes from its central woody stalk when it is growing. A scape is a thin green extension of the stalk that forms a 360-degree curl with a small bulbil, or swelling, several inches from its end. Inside the bulbil are more than 100 tiny cloves that are genetically identical to the parent bulb beneath. Many people call these "flowers," but they are not really blooms. If left on the plant, the scape will eventually die and fall over, and the tiny cloves will spill onto the ground. However, most never make it that far.

Cutting off the scapes keeps the plant's energy from forming the bulbil and therefore encourages larger bulbs. But don't throw out the scapes. They can be a delicious ingredient in your cooking.

GARLIC LOVERS UNITE!

The annual Gilroy Garlic Festival in Gilroy, California, invites you to celebrate this "palate-pleasing herb" during the last full weekend of July. The festival debuted in 1979 and has grown into an incredible event. In 2005, the festival hosted nearly 130,000 people, involved the work of 4,000 volunteers, and raised more than $300,000 for 170 local charities.

This famous festival also boasts a garlic cook-off that begins in December with a call for great garlic recipes and ends with finalists preparing their dishes in front of the crowd in July. Entertainment, arts, crafts, and dozens of delectable garlic dishes await festival attendees. For more information, visit the festival Web site at www.gilroygarlicfestival.com.

Can't make it to California? Take heart—there are many smaller garlic festivals, too. An Internet search for "garlic festivals" will yield hundreds of events, some of which are probably in your area.

There are three main types of hardneck garlic:

Rocambole. This variety has a rich, full-bodied taste. It peels easily and typically has just one set of cloves around the woody stalk. It keeps for up to six months.

Porcelain. Porcelain garlic is similar to rocambole in flavor and typically contains about four large cloves wrapped in a very smooth, white, papery sheath, but don't confuse it with elephant garlic, which also has large cloves. Porcelain garlic stores well for about eight months.

GARLIC'S FAMILY TREE

Family: Liliaceae

The lily family contains more than 4,000 species, including common garden flowers such as daylilies and trillium. Some botanists now classify *Alliums* into their own family, *Aliaceae*.

Genus: Allium (includes garlic, onions, leeks, scallions, chives, and shallots)

Species: Allium sativum (cultivated garlic)

Varieties: hardneck and softneck

Subvarieties:

HARDNECK	SOFTNECK
rocambole	artichoke
porcelain	Asiatic
purple stripe	turban
marbled purple stripe	silverskin
glazed purple stripe	silverskin Creole

Purple stripe. This hardneck variety is famous for making the best baked garlic. There are several types of purple stripe, all with distinctive bright purple streaks on their papery sheaths. Purple stripe garlic keeps for about six months.

Another member of the *Allium* clan, elephant garlic (*Allium ampeloprasum*), may look like a good buy because it is so large, but its flavor is very bland. Elephant garlic tastes more like a leek; in fact, its garlic flavor is slight and its healing properties are inferior to those of other garlic varieties. Use elephant garlic more like a vegetable than a flavorful herb.

The Brightest Bulb

Once you've decided which variety of garlic to use, consider the following tips to find that perfect bulb:

- Select bulbs that are completely dry.
- Choose bulbs whose cloves are plump and firm.
- Look for plenty of papery sheath.
- Avoid soft or crumbly cloves; spongy or shriveled cloves; bulbs or cloves with green shoots (they are past their prime); and preminced garlic, which has a weak flavor.

Growing Garlic

It's easy to grow your own garlic. It's hardy, tolerates cold weather well, and does not need pampering. Whether in a garden or a patio pot, garlic grows well under most conditions and requires little maintenance.

Many gardeners, especially those in northern climates, plant their garlic in October. Others prefer to do it on the shortest day of the year—the winter solstice in December. Planting in the fall lengthens the growing time so bulbs get a jump start on spring and can grow larger. Some gardeners in more southern climates prefer to plant garlic four to six weeks before the date of the last frost.

Garlic is robust enough to survive the frigid months, but if the winter seems too cold or the snow doesn't form a thick enough blanket over the plants, you can cover the bulbs and emerging shoots with straw or other mulching material for insulation.

You can try planting the garlic you buy from your local grocery store, but some grocery store garlic is treated with a sprout inhibitor that disrupts the natural growing cycle. If you don't know whether your store-bought garlic is treated this way, visit a plant nursery or garden center to purchase naturally grown garlic that is suitable for gardening. If you prefer to try your hand with specialty garlics, visit a garden center or check a seed catalog.

How to Plant

To plant garlic, gently remove the outer skin from the entire bulb and separate the individual cloves, taking care not to damage them. (Leave in place the thin papery skin that covers each clove.) Choose eight to ten of the largest cloves from the outside of the bulb for planting.

Place the cloves in the ground, tip up, in a place that gets about six hours of direct sunlight per day. Garlic needs to grow quickly to form large bulbs, and full sun fosters fast growth. You'll also want to be sure the area in which you plant will not become waterlogged in winter.

Work the soil about ten inches deep, adding organic matter and perhaps even sand to improve drainage. Bury the cloves in this loose, fertile soil so the tips are about two inches beneath the surface of the soil and the cloves are four to six inches apart. Apply a weak organic fertilizer every two weeks or so. Water the plants regularly so the soil is moist but not overly soggy, and pluck out weeds that would otherwise compete for nutrients and possibly over-grow the garlic.

Garlic prefers hotter and drier conditions as it matures. If you water the garlic less frequently near the end of the growing season, it will dry out a bit and its flavor will be better. Of course, the amount of water your garlic needs

Plant Pals

Many gardeners firmly believe in companion planting—the idea that some plants prefer certain kinds
of "company" to others. When these plants grow next
to plants they "like," they seem to fare better and
have improved flavor. Some plants emit odors that
protect others against particular pests. Scientists
aren't completely certain why these relationships
work (most are not scientifically proven), but many
long-time gardeners swear by them.

Garlic deters pests, so plant it liberally throughout the
garden. It may discourage aphids, nibbling insects,
and even snails and slugs. As an added bonus, planting
garlic near herbs is said to enhance their essential oils.

Avoid planting garlic near peas, potatoes, or legumes,
however, because these plants don't do well when
planted next to garlic.

depends on your area's climate, so keep a close eye on
your soil.

Harvesting Garlic

It's time to harvest your garlic when the green tops dry out
and turn yellow-brown. This is typically about three to
four months into the growing season—late summer or
early fall. Some gardeners prefer to harvest their garlic on
the longest day of the year—the summer solstice in June.
Harvest too early, and you get small bulbs. Harvest too late,

Your Guide to Planting Garlic

When: Plant either in the fall or four to six weeks before the last frost.

Where: Plant in loose, fertile, well-drained soil that gets about six hours of direct sun daily.

How: Set cloves point up, two inches deep and at least four inches apart.

Water: Provide ample water throughout the growing season and less water as plants mature.

Fertilizer: Apply mild organic fertilizer every two weeks.

Harvest: When tops turn yellow and dry out, dig up the entire plant.

and the bulbs may split. This indicates that they have already started their next growing season and diminishes their culinary quality.

Before you harvest all your plants, carefully dig up one bulb and examine it. Check its size, and count the layers of papery skin. If the bulb seems well formed, the cloves are plump, and there are about three layers of papery covering, harvest your crop. If there are four or more layers, let the plants grow a bit longer. When you're ready to harvest, use a small garden trowel to loosen the soil around each bulb. Then dig up the entire plant and shake off loose soil.

Some gardeners save part of their crop for planting again. Others believe that doing so heightens the risk of disease and results in smaller bulbs the next year. Because you can easily buy garlic to plant at a garden center, there may not be a need to save any cloves, unless you cultivate unusual varieties.

STORAGE

Storing your garlic in favorable conditions helps to maintain its healing properties and flavor. Properly stored garlic can last for months, ensuring that you always have some on hand for the next recipe.

"Young wet," or "new season," garlic is an immature garlic that is harvested in early summer. Immature garlic needs to be stored in the refrigerator and used within a week or so. It has a fresh, mild taste and can substitute for onions and leeks or lend a subtle garlic flavor to a recipe. Some cooks consider this the best, most flavorful garlic. As an added bonus, it may be more easily digested than dry garlic. Experiment with some of this "fresh" garlic and see how you like it.

You'll need to dry your homegrown garlic before you store it for a prolonged time. After harvesting, carefully wash the bulb and roots. Let the garlic dry in a shady, well-ventilated, moisture-free area for a week or more. You can hang the freshly harvested bulbs from their stalks if you like. Thoroughly drying garlic bulbs develops and concentrates their flavor, so don't rush the process. Once dry, trim or break off the roots and rub off the outer layer of parchment. If you've grown softneck garlic, consider braiding it for an attractive storage option.

Whole bulbs of store-bought garlic will keep for several months or more when stored at room temperature in a dry, dark place that has ample air circulation. Keep in mind, however, that garlic's lifetime decreases once you start removing cloves from the bulb. Storing garlic uncovered, such as in a wire-mesh basket inside your cupboard or beneath a small overturned clay pot, is ideal. You can also store garlic in a paper bag, egg carton, or mesh bag. Just be sure there is plenty of dry air and little light to inhibit sprouting. To avoid mold, do not refrigerate or store garlic in plastic bags.

If you've prepared more garlic than you need for a particular recipe, you can store minced garlic in the refrigerator in an air-tight container. Although the most active sulfur compound diminishes within a few hours, refrigeration will slightly slow the process. Use refrigerated garlic as soon as possible. Some people are tempted to freeze garlic, but this is not recommended because its texture and flavor change in extremely cold conditions.

GARLIC IN THE KITCHEN

The first thing to remember about cooking with garlic is the difference between bulbs and cloves. The average teardrop-shape garlic bulb is about two inches wide and two inches tall. It typically contains about 10 to 20 individual cloves about the size of your thumbnail. Most recipes call for one or more *cloves*, not *bulbs*.

To separate the individual cloves from the bulb, place the bulb on a flat surface. Use the heel of your hand to apply firm but gentle pressure at an angle. The parchment layers will separate, allowing you to carefully remove as many cloves as you need. Then, tenderly remove the thin covering on each individual clove. Most people reach for the plumpest cloves, but the smaller cloves have a more intense flavor.

Because one of garlic's most beneficial ingredients, allicin, is partially destroyed by cooking, you'll get the greatest health boost if you use it raw or only lightly cooked when you can. However, cooking garlic forms other healthy sulfur compounds, so you still receive benefits when you cook it. Plan ahead so you can cut, crush, or chop your garlic and let it sit for 15 minutes or more before using it, to activate the enzymes that turn alliin into allicin.

EASY PEELING

To easily peel garlic, slice off each end of a clove. Then, turn your broad chef's knife sideways so the flat side is parallel to your cutting board and the sharp edge is facing away from you. Place your knife this way on top of the clove and give the blade a quick pop with the heel of your hand to lightly crush the garlic clove (you don't want to mash it). The papery skins then rub off easily.

If you're going to peel many garlic cloves at once, drop them into boiling water for 10 to 20 seconds. Then plunge them into cold water. The skins will slide right off between your thumb and forefinger.

GIDDY FOR GARLIC
AROUND THE GLOBE

Garlic adds the spice of life to foods in countries all around the world. Along with ginger and onions, garlic flavors many of the foods of Southeast Asia. Teamed with tahini, it makes Middle-Eastern foods dining delights. Combined with chili peppers, garlic adds spark to Latin cuisine. Feel free to add garlic's robust flavor to your favorite recipes to take advantage of its healing benefits.

THE FLAVOR OF FORCE

Whether you rule garlic with a gentle or firm hand determines the amount and type of flavor you get. Here are some taste tips:

* Gently peel and use cloves whole to impart just a hint of garlic flavor.

* Slice cloves lengthwise for mild flavor or for long-cooking dishes.

* Mince cloves for medium flavor or for your quick-cooking dishes.

Firmly push cloves through a garlic press for the strongest flavor. If you don't have a garlic press, put your knife to work and finely chop the garlic. Remember, the smaller the pieces, the more pungent the flavor. Sprinkle the chopped garlic with a bit of salt, because salt pulls out liquid from the chopped garlic. Then firmly rub the salted chopped garlic with the side of your knife blade, further crushing it.